Cello Time Runners

a second book of easy pieces for cello

Kathy and David Blackwell

illustrations by Alan Rowe

Grateful thanks are due to Polly Chilcott, Alison Ingram, Avril Ivin, Tom Morter, and Janet Parsons for all their help with this volume.

Welcome to **Cello Time Runners**. You'll find:

- pieces using 2nd finger
- pieces using backward and forward extensions
- semiquavers, dotted crotchets, and 6/8 time
- duets, with parts of equal difficulty
- scales and arpeggios covering the keys you'll find in the book, plus G major 2 octaves
- Music Fact-Finder Pages at the back to help explain words and signs
- CD with performances of all the pieces to play along to. Pieces counted in; drumkit added for the jazz and rock numbers
- straightforward piano accompaniments available in a separate volume

MUSIC DEPARTMENT

OXFORD
UNIVERSITY PRESS

1. Start the show
(for Clare)

Printed by Halstan & Co. Ltd., Amersham, Bucks., England

OXFORD UNIVERSITY PRESS, MUSIC DEPARTMENT, GREAT CLARENDON STREET, OXFORD OX2 6DP

2. Banyan tree

Jamaican

3. Heat haze

4. Medieval tale

4

5. Chase in the dark

Count 2 bars

With menace

6. Spy movie

7. Gypsy dance

Work on L.H.

8. Pick a bale of cotton

9. On the go!

10. That's how it goes!

Luckily this piece is not as hard as it looks!

11. Blue whale

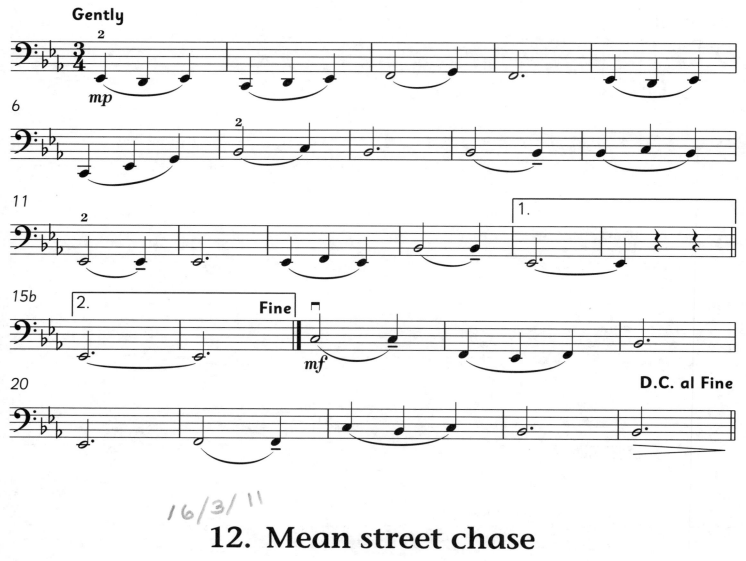

16/3/11

12. Mean street chase

ta te-te te te te

10

13. Allegretto

Mozart

14. Cornish May song

Traditional

15. Noël

Daquin

16. Prelude from 'Te Deum'

Charpentier

17. Paris café

18. Starry night

19. Cello Time rag

String Time Joggers

14 pieces for flexible ensemble

By Kathy and David Blackwell

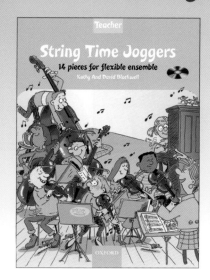

This exciting new series by the authors of *Fiddle Time, Viola Time*, and *Cello Time* provides great new ensemble material for all string groups, whatever their size. *String Time Joggers* is a must-have for all those looking for imaginative and enjoyable ensemble repertoire.

- 14 fun and characterful ensemble pieces—arranged in suites for concert performance
- Flexible scoring for violin, viola, cello, and double bass with piano or CD accompaniment—from two parts to massed string ensemble!
- Pieces may also be played as solos for violin, viola, or cello, with piano or CD backing
- Lively illustrations in the pupils' books
- Corresponds to the level of *Fiddle Time Joggers, Viola Time Joggers*, and *Cello Time Joggers*—part 1 uses all fingers, part 2 uses 0-1 only.

Teacher's pack
Teacher's pack includes full score, piano score, notes on the pieces, and CD with performances and backing tracks
978-0-19-335916-1

Violin book with CD
978-0-19-335913-0

Viola book with CD
978-0-19-335914-7

Cello book with CD
978-0-19-335915-4

Double bass part excl. CD
978-0-19-335970-3

You can look at and listen to pieces from the String Time Joggers books at
www.oup.com/uk/music/stringtime

OXFORD

Fiddle Time

By Kathy and David Blackwell

Fiddle Time Starters
978-0-19-322081-2

Fiddle Time Joggers with CD
A first book of very easy pieces for violin
978-0-19-322089-8

Fiddle Time Runners with CD
A second book of easy pieces for violin
978-0-19-322095-9

Fiddle Time Sprinters with CD
A third book of pieces for violin
978-0-19-322096-6

Fiddle Time Scales 1
Pieces, puzzles, scales, and arpeggios
978-0-19-322078-2

Fiddle Time Scales 2
Musicianship and technique through scales
978-0-19-322098-0

Fiddle Time Christmas with CD
A stockingful of 32 easy pieces
978-0-19-336933-7

Also available:

Joggers Piano Book	978-0-19-322119-2
Runners Piano Book	978-0-19-322120-8
Sprinters Piano Book	978-0-19-332097-3
Christmas Piano Book	978-0-19-337226-9

Praise for **Fiddle Time:**

'Lively original pieces are mingled with well-known pieces and duets that build confidence every step of the way and are great fun to play.'

'The bright and joyful colourful cover is an immediate incentive to even the most jaded young person to open this book and discover its musical delights.'

Stringendo (AUSTA Journal)

'An excellent collection in every way.'

Music Teacher

These books can be used with mixed string groups:

Fiddle Time Joggers is compatible with *Viola Time Joggers*.

Fiddle Time Runners is compatible with *Viola Time Runners*.

You can look at and listen to pieces from the Fiddle Time books at
www.oup.com/uk/music/stringtime

20. Caribbean sunshine

21. Jacob's dance

22. Song from the show

23. The road to Donegal

Can also be bowed: ♩ ♪♩ ♩ ♪♩ | etc.

24. Cat's eyes

25. Mexican fiesta

Use these words to help with the rhythm:

Tro - pi - cal   heat-wave   in   Mex - i - co

26. Summer evening

27. Extension rock

28. Show off!

22

29. You and me

You and me!

30. One day

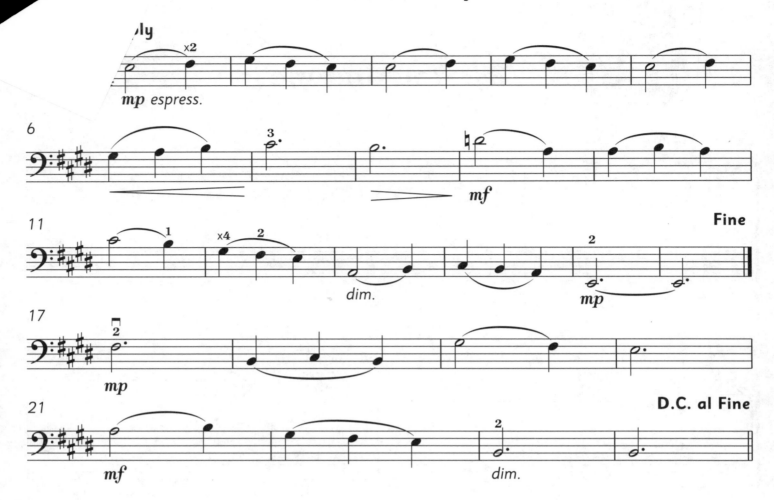

31. Aerobics

32. Hungarian folk dance

33. Show stopper

34. Farewell to Skye

(for Iain)

Scaley Things

C major scale 2 octaves

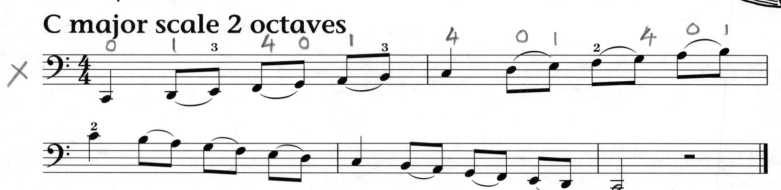

C major arpeggio 2 octaves

F major scale 1 octave

F major arpeggio 1 octave

Bb major scale 1 octave

Bb major arpeggio 1 octave

D major scale 2 octaves

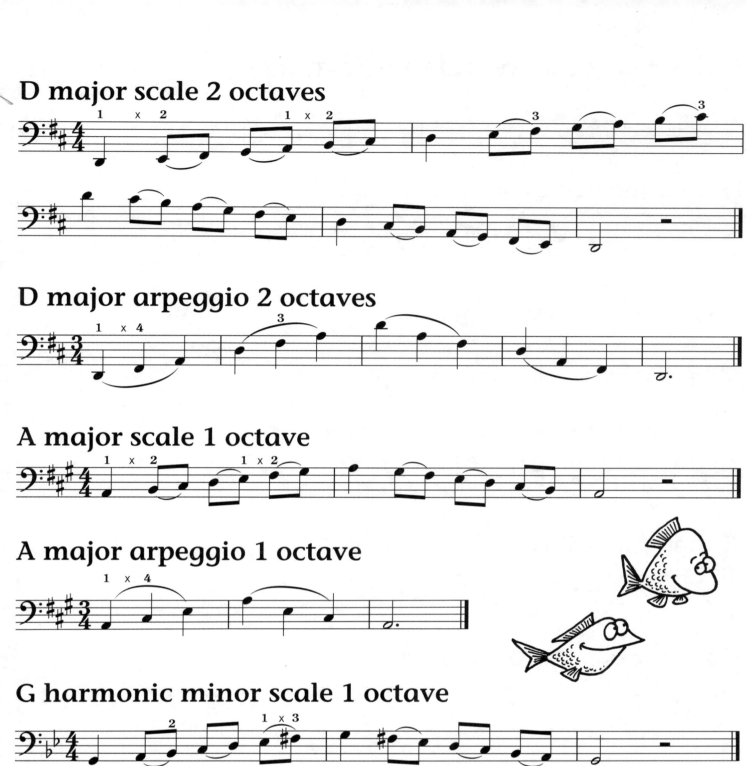

D major arpeggio 2 octaves

A major scale 1 octave

A major arpeggio 1 octave

G harmonic minor scale 1 octave

G melodic minor scale 1 octave

G minor arpeggio 1 octave

D harmonic minor scale 1 octave

D melodic minor scale 1 octave

D minor arpeggio 1 octave

C harmonic minor scale 1 octave

C melodic minor scale 1 octave

C minor arpeggio 1 octave

G major scale 2 octaves

G major arpeggio 2 octaves

Music Fact-Finder Pages

Here are some of the strange words and signs you will find in some of your pieces!

How to play it

pizzicato or pizz. = pluck

arco = with the bow

⊓ = down bow

V = up bow

> = accent

gliss. (glissando) = slide your finger along the string

Don't get lost!

‖: :‖ = repeat marks

| 1. | 2. | = first and second time bars

Play the first bar first time through; skip to the second bar on the repeat

D.C. al Fine = repeat from the beginning and stop at **Fine**

D.℠. al Fine = repeat from the sign ℠ and stop at **Fine**

rit. or **rall.** = gradually getting slower

molto rall. = slow down a lot

a tempo = back to the first speed

⌢ = pause

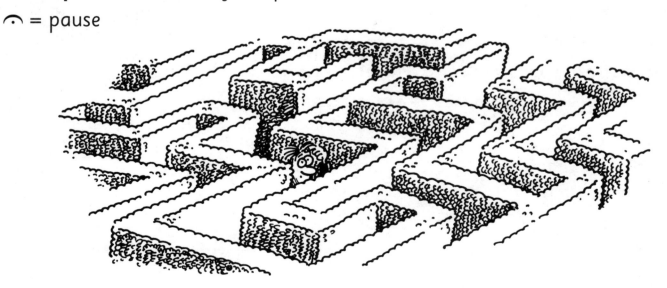

Volume control

p (*piano*) = quiet

mp (*mezzo-piano*) = moderately quiet

mf (*mezzo-forte*) = moderately loud

f (*forte*) = loud

ff (*fortissimo*) = very loud

———————————————— or *crescendo* (*cresc.*)

= getting gradually louder

———————————————— or *diminuendo* (*dim.*)

= getting gradually quieter

Italian phrase-book

accelerando = gradually get faster

Allegro = fast and lively

Allegretto = not too fast

Andante = at a walking pace

espress. = expressively

legato = smoothly

Maestoso = majestically

Moderato = at a moderate speed

staccato = short

Practissimo = lots of Cello Time!